Missing You, Metropolis

Missing You, Metropolis

Gary Jackson

Winner of the 2009 Cave Canem Poetry Prize
Selected and Introduced by Yusef Komunyakaa

GRAYWOLF PRESS

This publication is made possible by funding provided in part by a grant from the Minnesota State Arts Board, through an appropriation by the Minnesota State Legislature, a grant from the National Endowment for the Arts, and private funders. Significant support has also been provided by Target; the McKnight Foundation; and other generous contributions from foundations, corporations, and individuals. To these organizations and individuals we offer our heartfelt thanks.

Published by Graywolf Press
212 Third Avenue North, Suite 485
Minneapolis, Minnesota 55401
All rights reserved.

www.graywolfpress.org

Published in the United States of America

ISBN 978-1-55597-572-2

8 10 12 14 13 11 9 7

Library of Congress Control Number: 2010922929

Cover design: KapoNg@A-men Project

for Gina and Stuart

Contents

Introduction

Gary Jackson's *Missing You, Metropolis* embodies a voice uniquely shaped and tuned for the twenty-first century. Playful, jaunty, rueful, and highly serious—sometimes within a singular poem—this persona has been forged in the cauldron of popular iconography, especially in the culture of the comic book. Anything is possible in such created time and space; immediate tension exists in a climate where otherworldly figures are defined by earthly matters and concerns. The funny-book world is a perfect landscape for innuendo and signification, and Jackson uses these aptly. This first collection of poems is gauged by a sophisticated heart. Pathos breathes slightly underneath the visual comedy, and this quality is the true genius of *Missing You, Metropolis*.

These poems are American to the core. Though the characters in this saga of images don't wear "Made in America" logos on their foreheads, we easily recognize them, if not as prototypes, then at least as psychological facsimiles for our daily obsessions. Metropolis is a place in our psyche tooled by dreams and wishful thinking, where secret oaths are gladly taken; each nuance and gesture seems to reflect the concerns of the cultural architects of *nowness*, but this place is also a community of proper names, aliases, and familial ghosts. The main speaker in these poems knows all the nooks and crannies of a territory that is summoned repeatedly through an acute longing. One also feels that a speaker may miss his or her physical landscape as intensively as lost souls may come to populate a place merely through imagination. These proxies do know something about living and dying as they collide with each other (often in the attitude of pleasure-seeking androids), but they also know how to cajole and weep. This collection captures the anguish and pathos often associated with the complexity of today's human existence, which seems to be doubly troublesome in an era of technological adroitness and fluency. *Missing You, Metropolis* is an act of conjuring; it is a restive for confronting loneliness in a world of sped-up motion that seems devoid of mature emotion. This psychologically enhanced virtual reality, for the reader, grows into a twenty-first-century neo-surrealism. Indeed, some of the characters here are capable of a verbal shuck-and-jive, but there's always a human dimension to their hearts and minds. And, at times, the actors here may not be the most sober reflections, but somehow we still commiserate with them as we query and scrutinize this fun house of varied dimensions. And we even dare ourselves to love them because we realize that we are them.

Many of the poems in *Missing You, Metropolis* embrace the personal dimension of social politics and rituals. Though we are drawn into a landscape of action figures and supernaturalism, the individual often seems magnified and simultaneously reduced—made more vulnerable. Perhaps it is what he or she is measured against. The action figures are often refashioned into sidekicks and soulmates—lovable and momentarily indestructible, and at times totally contradictory. This device creates tension throughout *Missing You, Metropolis.* What would art be without its moments of constructed and negotiated tension? That is one of many questions answered in the fascinating world of this challenging collection of poems by Gary Jackson. Welcome to an edgy state of mind called Metropolis, a place where the pleasure principle is alive and well on the borders of middle America.

Yusef Komunyakaa

Missing You, Metropolis

All those brilliant and resourceful sleuths and heroes offered a glimpse of a perfect world where morality worked the way it was meant to. Nobody in Doc Savage's world ever killed themselves except thwarted kamikaze assassins or enemy spies with cyanide capsules. Which world would you rather live in, if you had the choice?

—Hollis Mason from *Under the Hood* (Watchmen)

one

The Secret Art of Reading a Comic

(after Auden)

The old comics were never wrong.
Right always defended
by the hero—polished like Adonis.
In one moment Thor is paused
in flight toward his foe,
the motion lines steadying
his resolve as he hurtles
ever closer. The next moment
Mjolnir, his mystical hammer, slams
against the Black Knight's helmet
with a *thwack* in red letters—
emulating pain, as Thor announces
every move in white bubbles.

These are treats, delicious twenty-two-page
snacks we swallow, never questioning
the action between the panels' gutters
and how similar that world bleeds
into our own. Take, for example,

Avengers #4 where we see
the final days of World War II.
Captain America and his sidekick
Bucky chase a runaway plane.
As they grab hold, the plane explodes.
Cap yells *No!* cuing the combustion
of smoke and flame. The next panel
flashes forward twenty years. We see
Cap preserved in a glacier, found
by Iron Man, Giant Man and the others.
Hail the returning hero.

But what we don't see
before the miraculous resurrection
is Cap losing his grip on the plane,
falling and helpless
to watch Bucky
fragment into pieces.
And how below, the Allies carried on,
killing Nazis, failing
to notice the body wrapped
in the American flag, dropping
into the frigid ocean behind.

Stuart

We hung out in fifth grade
because we both enjoyed the curves
of comic-book women,
the rustle of cheap paper between fingers,

The 350th *Amazing Spider-Man* issue
featuring Dr. Doom.
Comics bonded us.
Or perhaps it goes further back?

Blacks were still rare
on our street, while whites
filled the neighborhood like dead
leaves in pool water.

We emerged into the world
in the same room:
our mothers' friendship triggered
by our simultaneous birth.

We had a comic origin, our coincidence
too significant to be ignored. We were
Batman and Robin, Captain America
and Bucky—not created to be singular.

But no one is.   Consider
how we enter this world, not alone,
but with someone
only a scream away.

After the Green

Mom joked *Both my children are special*
after I entered gifted. I didn't understand
what my sister did at school, only that at home
she couldn't play outside. Her body ticked

like a broken watch, arms moving staccato,
muscles jerking limbs to their own order.
Once, I stopped by her class,
saw the students chewing blocks,

throwing crayons, flailing in indoor
pools filled with cotton and straw.
The classroom noise wasn't the usual
chatter of children, instead a fragmented

moan that made me
ashamed to see her among them.

Mom only worried how the white boy
with water on the brain and drool
looked at my sister with longing.
Keep an eye on that boy.

One morning, as I stood in class,
memorizing a speech for the Optimist
Oratorical Speech Contest, mom, failing
to wake my sister, held her body until . . .

I can still smell pacifiers, formula milk,
crayons, baby powder. I'd like to think
I can still find her world
if I trace the right lines

in my mother's voice, the month of May.
But I can never stay long. Even now

when I think of her, I am filled
with a hollow rage. When all you can do
is watch a body fail,
what words are there?

The day after, my mother said,
She lived until she was eight. She proved
the doctors wrong by seven years.
As if this were a good thing.

Pretend

You're the mother, I'm the dad,
and your collie is our daughter,
our little Jessica, the most beautiful

light-skinned baby in Topeka.
She's sleeping under the swings.
I want to take you to the movies,
so I call the babysitter.

We ride our bikes around
the block and sit on someone's
front porch eating air,

watching the show, holding
hands. You move in
so close we can smell
the salt on our breaths.

Your mother's voice echoes
down the block and brings you back
into the neighborhood, away

from the theater with me.
You glance at your neon-green watch
that howls on every hour like a basset
and check the silence.

Soon we'll be neighbors again,
and we'll decide we're too old
to play these games. But tonight

you stare at me as if we're still
pretending. You turn, pedal, thread
between street lights, chrome
handles catching dusk.

In a Conversation about Superheroes

Matt says Mystique,
because she can take any form.
We have to admit
she's a trump card.
What better woman
than someone who can become
any ex or future lover?

Jim says the Invisible Woman.
We imagine the feel of soft air
like Kansas clouds in fall.
But Jim claims seeing his own dick
inside her is a sight
he can't afford to pass up.

They groan when I say Storm.
She's boring because she's only
black. Although she has
white hair, blue eyes,
taller than a lightpost
and can control the weather,
they know I've picked her
for her skin alone.

Stuart surprises us
when he says Shadowcat.
She can pass through
solid objects. How fun
could she be? But Stuart
knows how she works.

How she could nestle
under his skin. Slip
herself around him like gray
sky around rain.

Cornell

was an asphalt nigger. Even in first grade
he had a crew of hardknocks.
During dodgeball they always threw
the ball a few feet too short

so it would roll into his hands.
And we always scattered
too late. He was our executioner,
able to turn our black skin blue.

In junior high, we trained him
not to bite the hand that feeds.
Offered him blunts, gold chains,
anything to point him at someone

besides ourselves. But without him,
someone new would come,
just as willing to punish his own
for being near. And we all

wanted to bleed someone,
but there was no one else close
enough to cut. Once,
while I was skipping sixth hour

in the parking lot, he pulled up,
six-deep, in an '84 Lincoln Continental
and hollered my name. The word was
he killed three boys that week.

I walked to his window,
rolled down to let the smoke tumble out,

revealing the worn faces
inside. He asked one question.
I shrugged, shook my head.
      Before I could step away

he was already pulling off.
Even if I had weed to give,
I'd save it for myself. For those days
when going home isn't enough.

There's always someone waiting
to bring back all the old fears—black fists
slamming like stones into black bodies,
tearing the meat to the bone.

The Family Solid

We were barely out
of middle school
when Stuart showed me the scar—
an S branded in his brown arm.
Solid, Stuart said, fresh
from his initiation.
They held him down
in a basement, seared his skin.

He wanted another family.
One that encouraged his want
for the blood of possibility,
that heart-pumping rage
that wraps us in a noose,
impossible to untie.

We have ties to Bloods.
I didn't need that family,
had heard enough stories
about my father,
how when I was seven
months old, three men came to his home
in Inglewood. He pleaded
with them to let his mother,
girlfriend and son go before
they did whatever
they were going to do.

When Stuart told me
My niggas can hold me down,
the image of him in darkness,
pinned by three strangers,
burned into my mind.
Like the white-hot needle
as it pierces skin.

The ending, I no longer
remember, but the desire died
and he escaped. Surprising,
I know, but black kids
find a way out without
getting locked up or put down.

Years later, he'd absently rub
his scarred skin like an itch.
The S on his bicep
lingering above the blood.

Kansas Winter Blues

We wanted to impress one of those girls you took in the dark
room that morning to talk and kiss among photos

of football games and faculty profiles. After school,
she'll bring a friend and we'll drive around town before going

home. The four of us will pass around the Hennessy hidden
in your backpack until we all feel loose and eager

to touch. But instead, we're chatting in news lab
under the user names *YHVH* and *Wolverine* with girls

in Dublin and Melbourne, wondering how they sound
on all fours, preferring words over flesh.

Now it's after five, your girl isn't here, your car won't start,
so we walk home in the middle of February.

The snow goes out of its way to fall into ears and under
jacket collars as we talk of how we'll leave this state and stumble

between some woman's legs who'll never grow old or tired
of loving us, despite our diet of Snickers, comics, and porn.

At home we'll log back on, chat with a few girls, while we hold
the frost in our lungs, waiting for someone to come.

Natalie Pays the Neighbor Boy a Visit

I needed a shot of Everclear, a joint,
something to help enjoy you.
If I was to be your first,
I knew it wouldn't take long.

Since you hadn't yet learned
to squeeze without hurting,
I left my shirt on.
But you did, at least, get me
that shot. And when I was halfway
off the couch—your body
the only thing keeping me on—
I wanted to slow you down.

You were always a sweet neighbor,
and though there was no appeal
(I had been with black guys before,
but lied for your pride),
you were always curious to me,
as if you never shut off your mind.

When you told me
you wanted to get your first
out of the way, I told myself,
it didn't matter
after you pulled out. If I wanted,
I'd have kept you a little longer,
teased all I could out of you,
trained you how to please a girl.

And maybe I would have,
if I was the girl who made you
stutter, the first girl you held
sweaty palms with, too nervous
to kiss, some sweet pudding
of a girl with tits like mine.

Saturday Mornings with Andrea True

After *Ninja Turtles* and *Darkwing Duck*
Stuart and I delved into the grocery sack
in my grandfather's closet and began our fling
with 70s pornography.
We used pillows to hide ourselves
while we watched women
grind on top of men.
Yet none of them were attractive—
sure we could see their lips and nipples,
but this, we feared, would get stale,
and soon these women would become
as interchangeable as any
of our junior high teachers.

When Stuart found *Sweet Wet Lips*
halfway through the stack,
he fell in love with the woman
who never spoke, who blew
bubble gum while men came on her
face. And she never popped
until she finished. He found her
name in the credits, kept it
in his mind for years,

found her online, ordered her,
invited me over. When we watched
Sweet Wet Lips we were kids again,
wrapped in the memory of bubble gum and sex.
He asked the names of the others.
I rattled off *Looking for Lust, Black Sister/
White Brother, The Big Bang.*
He bought them all, and even after

he died I saw in his room a brown paper bag
by the bed. His Aunt Hattie blushed,
Those are his dirty tapes.
I opened the bag, saw our childhood
in those old tapes—a stacked burial—
and offered to throw them away.

two

The Golden Avenger

Young boys listen to his adventures
with an uncanny ear. They act

alongside their radios and pretend
they wear a golden three-piece

with matching fedora
as they race down alleyways

after murderers and thieves.
Feel white-gloved fists hammer

jaws and chins. And when things
go wrong—as they always do—

they pull out the gun, shoot a single beam
of light, the kind that blinds

the ugliest of men, and proceed
to beat them. It's fiction,

an escape, something we only
dream of. But if someone felt

compelled to become the fantasy,
as long as he saved the right people,

who cares who he hurts?

Upon Seeing Spider-Man on My Way to Work

I saw the bastard webslinging over electric Soho,
miles above the stoplights and New Yorkers.

What I wouldn't give to be up there in some red-
and-blues, slingshotting between skyscrapers,

ready to swing in and save some beauty getting
mugged. I'd take out the thugs with an uppercut,

a flick of webs and a one-liner. But instead
I'm walking home in the goddamn New York

cold, because my car broke down and it's too
expensive to fix when you teach high school

and rent costs a grand. I wonder if Spider-Man
ever has to wait for traffic lights

or pedestrians, if the city is one slow crawl
below him. I'd trade my job, my BA,

hell even my wife, anything to climb walls,
spin webs, touch rooftops with toes.

Gothamites

Let Metropolis have its superman,
Keystone have its flash, Opal
its star. We have our Bat.
He is legend.

True he's only a man,
but not one boys dream about
becoming—streaking the cityscape,
freshly christened into godhood.
Our man keeps company
with gargoyles, skulks parapets,
keeps time by the flapping of wings.

We've heard the rumors—
from mutated bat
to millionaire playboy. How
he's fifty now, yet still keeps
stride with heroes able to pitch
the moon into the earth.

Some of us bet he's even
Gotham-grown, right here.
Not some Kryptonian
or clay breathed to life.
But one of us, who just decided
he was gonna right a few wrongs,
take this crime-fighting business
into his own hands,
show those other costumes
how a man defends his home.

Nightcrawler Buys a Woman a Drink

You're staring, jaw-dropped at my tail. And yes,
it's a good twenty inches long and moves

like a serpent in heat. Touch it. I'm no devil, honey,
I don't got no souls, just the smoothest, bluest fur

you've ever seen. Don't mind my buddy here, he looks angry
all the time, and he's got eyes for the bottle of Jameson

and the short-haired blonde playing pool near the gorillas.
What do we do? Over a few drinks I could tell you about the time

we traveled to the blue side of the moon or when we fought
the Juggernaut right here in this bar. Yeah, the fangs are real.

Rub your finger over them, touch the deviled tongue.
Caress my fur with your skin, let me keep your body warm

in the dark. It's your night, honey. Show me a woman not afraid
of a mutant man. Let me mix into your bloodline.

Listening to Plath in Poetics

I'm staring at your leather belt, praying
those jeans loosen their grip enough

to reveal your porcelain back while I listen
to "blacks crackle and drag." You

haven't caught me peering at the sliver of flesh
between jeans and shirt. The warm glisten

of your sweat rests on the only hint of skin
I can see. I've heard "Daddy" before,

I could be yours and you could be my Lady Lazarus
and eat me like air. And I would feed you a lie,

one of the little ones—the kind that turns
strangers to lovers, that turns words to poems.

Kansas Photo

LaToya, Stuart and I are standing
behind the apartment complex, snow erasing
the un-worked brown pockmarked acre
with a smooth layer of white, five inches deep.
 We have jackets on
posing side by side by side, untouched by the cold,
unsmiling, as if this is to be our debut album cover.
 Stuart, in Stuart-fashion, has his pants
pulled down to his ankles, belt buckle resting
in the snow, his blue boxers complementing
his ashy legs and stoic expression.
 Our bodies an ellipsis on the snow field:
leading us nowhere on a blank page.

How the Unstoppable Juggernaut
Makes a Living after Retirement

Cain Marko sits in the corner of Harry's Hideout,
arm-wrestling men forty years younger, smashing
each hand on ancient wood, pining for heroes.

When Cain was a villain, his partner—
Black Tom Cassidy—helped him fight the X-Men,
and they would have won, if not for

a trove of leprechauns. But the business
was never lucrative, and a body's gotta eat.
Tom stands nearby, taking bets. Men thrust money

into his hands, waiting like wolves. Cain earns
another eighty, nearly breaking a boy's wrist.
The next man takes his seat across from Cain

and downs his beer. He reminds Cain of someone
an age gone, with golden hair and muscles full like oceans.
Cain's right hand—Tom's moneymaker—falters

with the grief that carries nostalgia,
and his left raises thick eyeglasses
from his shirt pocket to his face.

He's back in Brooklyn, surrounded by heroes,
his hands crushing Hawkeye's spine,
before he's leveled by Thor's hammer.

At a bar, he sits—a firm woman on his firm lap—
fresh after a beating from Spider-Man,
who sank him in a block of wet cement.

In Nevada, a gray-skinned Hulk bounces him
out of the casino, throws a haymaker that Cain takes
to the face for counting cards.

What are you looking at, grandpa?

the young man asks. Cain frowns and says nothing,
discards the memories, before breaking
the young man's arm as it slams, against its will,

onto the table. The crowd erupts with laughter
as a boy enters Harry's with shoulders like hammers,
and puts a hundred against the old man.

Tom snatches the money, Cain pulls from his
bottle. The boy spits on splintered wood and the men
hold their breaths like children, witness.

A Poem for Jesse Custer

If Jesse Custer wrote a poem it'd drink Daniels
straight and spit, but never in front of a woman.

If Jesse Custer wrote a poem it wouldn't take shit
from any man with a hard-on for hitting women,
whether he be a preacher or his best friend.

A Jesse Custer poem would smoke Marlboros
with a silver Zippo, the words "Fuck Communism"
inscribed on the side, a gift
from the goddamn Duke himself.

A Jesse Custer poem would be a bad motherfucker.
It'd right all wrongs by beating any evildoer
to pulp with its mitts. Make 'em think twice
before burning crosses, beating children
or shooting another man's dog.

If someone started shit in heaven or hell,
Jesse Custer's poem would know.
Even if God Himself did the starting,
Jesse Custer's poem would shoot Him
dead between the eyes, sit on His throne
and tilt its Stetson over its brow.

When Loving a Man Becomes Too Hard

Over a bottle of Merlot, Mary Jane
confesses she sometimes makes Peter
wear the costume when they fuck,

because she likes to pretend
Spider-Man is her other lover.
Betty can't relate, because she's only

made love with Bruce.
The Incredible Hulk is too big
for their bed, and no woman

wants to see a pickle
inside her. Mary Jane
says she's always been curious

about Bruce, and envies
the thrill of sleeping with one man
and waking up next to another,

transformed. But Betty reminds her
that both their husbands

turn the morning after.
Mary Jane considers the image

of Peter slipping
one red-and-blue legging on
at a time in their bedroom,

the mask almost pulled over his face.
Some days he leans in,
over their bed, kisses her

with the part of him
that still belongs to her,
before covering even that,

replacing her man with a new one,
a man that belongs to New York
and its myriad of victims and villains.

Some days she doesn't even get
that last kiss. And she holds
his absence like a crutch.

A Beautiful Lie

I'll steal a stare across your thigh
and trace the small flaws that freckle
toward your heavenly hips.
I'll follow the implicit aroma
of you and whisper something

to stir the rich syrup inside.
You'll laugh at the absurdity of it,
yet you'll come wearing a summer
dress—the random color of dawn—

hiding the soft down of flesh underneath.
Beneath the smooth rust of skin
we will find something near to want.
It won't take long. First, a night over
with a bottle of pinot noir, suddenly

we're buying a brand new television
and new drapes to match the couch. One
dog—your mother's—and then another
to keep her company when we go

out. Things accumulate in our closet
until we're too lazy to throw them away:
last year's Halloween decorations, weight sets
we never used, a dress you bought
for a friend's wedding, which I didn't go to.

But I was never good at preserving you,
and all things erode: like ink
off a newspaper, rivers into canyons,
statues down to dusted feet.

You will lie turned away from me
in the twilight of December.
I'll watch the freckles of your shoulders
melt into your back, and like you,
I will wait for nothing to happen.

The Dilemma of Lois Lane

When you first showed me your secret,
the red S hidden beneath your shirt
all these years, I lost my mind.
God, just looking at you, thinking
how those eyes will never fade
or dull, how your hair will never uncurl
and fall away and how even though
you haven't worked out since living
on the farm, your body will always be
as solid as diamonds.

And yet I have to pretend those things
don't exist, that you'll always be
the Clark that steps on people's
shoes in elevators, the Clark
that spills coffee on the break
room floor. But you blow forest
fires out with those same breaths
I take into me when we kiss
and when you're tired you dip
into stars for afternoon naps.
And I don't know which man
is real. Sometimes,
when we're alone at home,
fixing dinner, you'll pretend
to wince when you cut yourself,
and I find myself hoping
that the tiniest drop of blood
will bloom on your finger.

Bleed

Stuart showed us his new drawing
penciled in blood on the back of a proof
to the guys in the scanning room.

Kirk smiled, shook his head as if it were crayon.
Yearbook plant supervisors encourage insanity

in their third shifters; it counts
time better than the hum of desktops, the whir
of presses—all things designed to maintain

order. We struggled to fulfill quotas, counting
pages like miles, as every year ticks away

the kids in yearbook photos stay the same age,
created by the same factory—
each year's model the same as last.

Photo after photo of girls posing in gymnasiums,
boys standing on manicured lawns,

all viewed under the fluorescent lights
of a windowless building where midnight
looks like morning. Perhaps that's why

we indulged these performances—why Mikey
once wore a wedding dress to work;

why Aaron would show up high on a few pills,
with a few more, willing to share; why
Stuart, with a pricked finger, simply said

It was an experiment to see what it was like.
And we all laughed amid stacks of book covers

and ruined film. Young men lost
among dust and relics in the dead night
believing blood divided us.

Origin of Memory

Memory's so treacherous. One moment you're lost in a carnival of delights . . . the next it leads you somewhere you don't want to go. Memories are what our reason is based upon. If we can't face them we deny reason itself.

—The Joker from *The Killing Joke*

Ever since the accident, I forgot
who I was. Falling into toxic waste
does something to a mind.

Most days I don't even mind
my marshmallow skin,
my avocado hair, my mouth

a razor smile.
But other days, I need something
to remember myself by. So I decide

to go to the Gotham Public Library,
check out a few books by Maurice Sendak,
kill everyone in the building

to clear my head. Watching a body lose
light is the only thing that gives rise
to memory like mercury.

I finish the last one with a knife
to give him a grin like mine
and a little lipstick to pretty

his slashed face.
I count the seconds between
his breaths, as my past takes shape.

Soon I remember fragments:
being booed offstage, my wife's smile
that showed too much gum,

reading *Where the Wild Things Are*
to my little girl on Christmas Eve.

Memory is in the killing.

But the past always slips loose
until I'm the only olive in the martini,
and I'm used to being dry.

If only I could remember
the moment before I fell in
and cast the old life off—

why I'm incomplete,
the crack in every smile,
the black globe in every eye.

Superman's Funeral

I walked down to Metro Ave to watch
the procession and found myself in front

of the crowds, close enough to touch
the heroes march, float and fly by.

Then came the onyx casket,
a bright red S burned deep into the top.

Wonder Woman was one of four pallbearers,
and I had never seen her in person—

her marbled cheeks, Amazonian stature,
the star-freckled shorts and golden lasso

drawing attention to those carousel hips.
She wasn't even crying. Maybe Amazons

didn't do that. I couldn't help it—
I reached out and glossed her bare

shoulder as she walked by.
She glanced, but never broke form.

I had to get out of there.
At Bastion's I drank a pint of Boulevard Wheat

(on tap for $2.50, advertised
as Superman's favorite beer,

though he didn't drink).
Allowed myself to think I had a shot

if I got in trouble at the right place
and right time. After all, if she likes

Superman's type, I got the black hair
and blue eyes, and for her—

I'd even do a spit curl.
I could rescue her from a superhero's life.

Or at least show her a man
willing to stay home, and wait for her

until she flies through the bedroom window
after a hard day's work with men

in rubber costumes, fighting
people dressed as animals and lunatics.

I'd pour her a glass of pinot grigio.
Ask her how her day was.

Iron Man's Intervention, Starring the Avengers

As if I can't have a drink
or two in the morning,
before risking my life
for people who don't
know my name.

As if I can't enjoy
a bottle of Chianti
and a smooth woman
when I'm not disarming
warheads in mid-flight
over the Atlantic.

As if the bottle of Johnnie
Walker you found, half-
empty, in my briefcase
implies I'm not capable
of defending New York
from shape-shifting, green
men from another world.

A man at Starbucks shoved
me during morning rush.
I stumbled over chairs,
fell. With my suit—
my marvelous iron prison—
I could pop his head with a flick
of one finger. But without it,
I'm just a man lost in the city.

Meanwhile you walk
down streets with a cowl
or cape the only difference
and you're transformed—
the man underneath as real
as the one slamming villains
into concrete. You think
I need a drink to get in
the suit. But you're wrong.

I need it to get out.

Missing You, Metropolis

> *It makes me think about Clark and how he'd handle*
> *the situation. Not just the bending steel and flying out.*
> *Clark could smile. That Boy Scout thing . . . but the boy*
> *doesn't have Clark. He has me.*
>
> —Batman from *Batman #608*

Tellers held by gunpoint hurry to open vaults
and registers. I'm face down on the cement floor,
checking my watch. By now Superman would be here

in a flash of blue and red and these thugs
wouldn't know what hit them. Instead the lobby
erupts in smoke and everyone covers their mouths

as Batman descends from above in black and gray
and a lemon yellow belt. And when he lands,
instead of a whirlwind of colors, he moves like tar.

I'm surprised he hasn't retired. But they can't seem
to dodge his hands, and their bullets always miss.
The smoke clears as he scans the room

full of tellers and bankers cowering on the floor.
What I wouldn't give for Superman's
ungloved hand to help me up, before flashing

a wink or smile to reassure me everything will be
alright. But Batman is grimace set in stone;
he tackles the ringleader—this hulking tree-stump

of a bastard. They collide like two boxers.
There is no heat vision melting through steel, no lift
of bodies into the stratosphere until they are only

specks set against clouds, no explosion of light
that heralds victory. There are only the wet sounds
of blood-soaked fists pounding flesh,

the image of black boots bludgeoning skin,
the onyx gleam of bat-shaped knives
as they puncture veins, giving blood to fantasy.

three

Watchmen

When we go through the doors and the alarms go off, I pull out
the receipt so security can see. They eye the contents
      in our arms and nod as they check the list and say nothing

as they give it back. Tony shakes his head. *Now all of these*
white people are watching us. We both know
      it doesn't matter. They'd look anyway, it's just

they have a new reason, one that makes them comfortable
in their fear. They'll take inventory of our shoes,
      jackets, faces and save this moment along with every other—

whenever our skin rises from the cream of this city.
Or maybe they're voyeurs:
      committing our bodies to memory—

recalling our ideal forms in private. For them
it's a simple thrill to peer behind the veil—
          observe how the other color lives.

Luke Cage Tells It Like It Is

Don't believe everything you read.
The exploits you find in my comic
are no more probable
than snow in Sunnyvale.
I'm not as black as you dream.

But a body has to make a living.
And I play the part
better than any. I know
the dangers of believing
every shade of black you see.

In this issue
there's a Mandingo of a man,
dark like olives,
voice as deep as a desert valley
in the dead of night. He smiles
as if he wants to bite your throat,
holds back his teeth
with those bubblegum lips
he can't help but lick, leaving
the thinnest film of saliva
on the surface.
He's slick
and he's bold
and he's everything you imagine he should be.

Sometimes, you want to be him,
want to see yourself in the silver gleam of his image
and other times you want to be wanted by him.

Crave his brand of desire,
his form of righteousness,
bringing a little black to the world
one *motherfucker* at a time.

No matter how three-dimensional he seems,
know that behind every *jive turkey* uttered
there is not a black mouth, but a white one,
one that dictates who he calls Nigger,
to temper the perfect tone of black.

This is the cruelest trick.
Even now, I'm defined by the borders
of my panels, the hue of sienna ink,
an assembly of lines, a rendering of man
splayed across your page.

Storm on Display

Step right up, ladies and gents, come witness the marvelous
wonder of a woman genetically confused.

Marvel's first black mutant with features
as white as the hands of her creator.

Come, see her almond skin,
no different from ours save a darker ink.

Gaze onto her furious blue eyes and silken white hair
that no amount of peroxide could emulate.

But don't step *too* close, for she
is a skilled thief from her years on Cairo's streets

and as a young girl,
stuck a man in the gut for touching her swarthy parts.

When she found she could wrap clouds around her finger,
the natives worshipped her like she was the Almighty.

We've brought her here, all the way from her home,
just to show you folks a true and authentic

African Goddess. For a small price, take her
home, show your friends this ebony beaut of a creature.

Autumn in Chestnut Falls

Sure, some of us felt sorry
when the Franklins moved.
But once their oldest boy
grew tentacles for arms
we couldn't help but keep away.
The way they slithered
alongside him, as if they had
a mind of their own, ready
to drain the blood from toddlers
who stumbled too close.
And that was before Lucille

found her Labrador flayed to the bone
in her backyard. But we should have
known that boy was trouble when
he got kicked off varsity for leaving
welts on everyone he tackled,
even though he could hold onto
a ball like nobody's business.

Home from Work, I Face My Newborn Mutant Son

I hold my six-pound baby boy
in my hands, pink as sand.
His skin is glass.

This is not a metaphor.
My wife did not hemorrhage alone
on our wood floor for metaphor.

Even now, he squirms—his small cries
are like the whine of well-worn brakes.
He cuts into my palms and slides

in the creased blood. I see
his tiny organs getting used to their work,
while my wife—bled out—grows cold.

What paper-bag test can this boy pass?
His skin reflects the white of my eyes.
And I know he cannot last.

        For a moment, before I drop him,
I wonder how he'd make it?
Even if his skin does harden—

to crystal, to diamond—it won't be
enough, and I could not bear the sight
of him hanging like an ornament,

a glass boy from a tree, or find him
cracked open, splintered in the street.
        As he shatters on the floor,

everything from his heart to lungs
freezes like the hands
of a wristwatch at ground zero.

A Solider Stands Guard at Alamogordo, New Mexico, during the Testing of the First Gamma Bomb

After the blast, I watched a man
run through the white sand,
leaving jade footprints
behind. He collapsed, burning
in front of the green sun.
The skin flayed
from his body, I could trace
every plum-colored muscle
with my eye; they glowed
like tomatoes on a table
when the kitchen light hits
them just right and you suddenly
want to eat one more than anything.
But it was when his chest heaved,
like a loaf of bread rising,
that I forgot my station,
gathered his quivering
in my arms, radioed for help,
and held him until
the men took him away.

How to Get Lynched on the Job

During lunch, 3:00 A.M. in front
of the vending machines, Stuart whispered

in Nicole's ear that he wanted to taste
her. She got the hell away,

he just laughed. It was the first time
I worried for him. Never mind

she was engaged. Never mind the harassment
suit that should've followed. She was white.

Whistling and whispering, it's all the same.
The truth is the world ain't changed.

None of us are far
from ending like Emmett.

Magneto Eyes Strange Fruit

Out for a midnight flight, I see
two children on the playground—

the rust of blood crusting
over holes in their heads.

Their brown bodies dance
like marionettes, tangled

in the swings. "Mutie"
is scrawled across the cardboard

that hangs from their swollen necks,
the chains wrapped tight enough to tear.

I imagine what they did,
maybe the ability to turn glass into sand,

to hear rustled leaves as words,
something simple, something

humans kill for. I reach out,
close the girl's eyes, and suddenly

I want to rip every man out of his home,
make each one burn, reverse

the earth's rotation, rupture the core
and tear this planet inside out,

only so they can know how it feels.
It's been so long since I've taught people

how to fear, since I've razed their cities,
bent steel and split iron into handfuls

of dust, but someone must be
the villain for the dead.

four

Machine

Stuart shows me the cross-like scars
on his wrists, proud of his curiosity.
He wanted to see how the veins
pulled it all together, hoping to make sense

of god's machine. Now I'm standing
with him in a room with two twin beds:
crayon children dancing on wooden frames.
I'm trying to make sense of my friend

in a place where people pace down
the halls because they can't write
with pencils or play the instruments
locked away in the rec room for fear

they'll cut themselves with dull lead
and nylon strings. As I exit
I hear the whine of speakers
announcing dinner: chicken breast

with green beans. Desperate to impart
some final words of empathy
that will convince him to stay with me,
I tell him it feels like a part of me

is in this place. He smiles.
A part of you is. Then laughs,
as if he realizes the world
has finally broken us
in two.

Confession from a Mutant Disco-Queen

I stand alongside the rooftop's edge
to watch the sun drown in her own red rays,
and I grow jealous of her color.

Once, I had my time in the spotlight. Called myself
Dazzler, wore white jumpsuits embedded with rhinestones
and transformed beat machines and ivory keys

into neon lightshows. I made crowds
swelter and swoon when I hit the colors
just right. I was born able to turn sound

into light. But my band leaked my gift to the press.
Suddenly I was Josephine Baker—and the spotlight
isn't enough to keep a woman warm in the dark.

So I moved back home, ran with the X-Men,
became a paralegal, went back to the stage.
I still get the occasional gig for a wedding or bat mitzvah,

but it's always the same. They just want to watch
my body glow like a disco ball while I sing soprano.
Even lovers beg for a few tricks. Wanting

me to push light from the inside,
so they can pretend they're in heaven.
Sometimes they kneel before me,

in mocking prayer. I wonder if they really see
something indescribable, one of those moments
like looking into the sun. I could blind them if I tried.

I take one foot, set it into the air. Every sound in the city
screams for attention. I take them all inside me, belt
oné long note to harmonize the color. Silence rolls

over the city like molasses on bread and I think
how fitting it'd be to fall right here, lit up like a goddamn star,
drawing every eye to this single point of light.

Xorn

*Sometimes the idea of the monster is
more real than the monster itself.*

—Professor Charles Xavier from
New X-Men (vol. 2) #127

My brain is a star. When I walk downtown, people don't run,
but walk fast. They know I'm a mutant, but the gravity

draws them near. Things got better once I laid my hands
on a woman. A car knocked her body in the air

like a heated molecule, and didn't bother to stop.
The crowd called the ambulance, but when they saw me—

my face bright as a halo, they believed
I was the second coming. I touched her.

They thought I brought her back, but I told them
I'm no Jesus. I simply take the good cells and fix them,

discard the dead ones like flicking ash into the air.
Now people won't leave me alone. I jump-start cars,

bring dead dogs to life, a girl brought me her dry goldfish.
How could I refuse?

I worked double-shifts for the emergency ward,
was even charged with healing the ozone,

but I couldn't get my hands on it.
Last week, a burgundy gargoyle galloped around town

and ate a few people on 56th and MLK.
They came out with shotguns and rifles to put him down.

They blew out his knees. I made my way
through the crowd, touched him, felt the pulse's warm glow,

like a maggot in the sun. He was a mutant
no older than three—in that phase children test the world

by tasting it; but when I told them he was an infant,
they still fired. I wondered

what his gift would have been.
A week later, a woman asked if I could bring back

her husband, who the boy had eaten. I told her
no, she slapped me, scorched her hand. Told me

I was a monster.
I told her there had to be something left

to raise, but she knew that. They all did or else
they wouldn't have burned the boy after they killed him.

I watched as their shadows, contorted by the flame's light,
danced into grotesque shapes with limbs like twigs,

jagged bodies, bitten apples for heads. They stomped
that boy's ash into the dirt and I longed to do more than heal.

Emergency

They released me today. At home
my mother is waiting and gives me
a fifty and a hug and

had to get back to Oklahoma.
Jim and Gary come by later.
Come walk with me.

We talk about the last girl I slept with
and how she's dealing. We don't
talk about ourselves.

Jim wants to see,
so I take off the bandages. A scar runs down
each wrist leaving a trail

of jagged skin in their wake.
Gary sees something
in the way I look
                    at those scars,

studying them.
            The road map buried
under flesh.   Later
            we pretend

nothing's wrong. But I'm living
in nostalgia—the moment I'm in
is already gone

and I'm looking   ahead
at the open
spread of trees

off 17th and Wanamaker and
it's not much farther   away.

I'm invited to stay
the night.   I imagine

         riding those veins
home,   tracing

their origin back to the heart—
         a violent muscle that threshes seventy beats
per minute   even at rest.

Jim has *Monster*
spinning   in the stereo
    and one more night is all
I have.

         Play me a song
before I go.

At home I take my aunt's keys,
         two bullets and
all the money I saved
              and find a pawn shop

still open down 17th and

I'm imagining those trees
                   again.
Six more minutes

till I park the car,
      escape into the gnarled

branches   of trees that all point
      toward the center
of old dirt under

the lights
   of dead stars.
                There's no moon
tonight   but I can still feel

the worn ivory
      grip.   Everything around me

used
     up.   One more
      use,
one   more

 night.
           Hurry,
before the sun

     shatters me

   to pieces.

Elegy for Gwen Stacy

> *Spider-Man appeared . . . . I knew he would save her.*
> *That was what they did. They saved innocents.*

—Phil Sheldon from *Marvels #4*

I can't stop dying.
The first time was 1973—
fell off the Brooklyn Bridge,
killed by my lover
as he tried to catch me
with his webs.
It was an accident,
he didn't understand terminal
velocity, sudden stops, whiplash.
It wasn't the Green Goblin
who killed me, or the falling,
but my hero.

Some people never forget
the way you laugh
or the way your body burns
as you walk away.
People never forgot the way
I died. They told their friends,
reread those issues
until the staples fell out
and fingerprints dulled the covers.
I died a lot in 1987.
Peter got married that same year.

I still get thank-you letters
from people who claim

if it wasn't for me,
they would have closed
this world off, abandoned it
like so many highway gas stations.
But it's not me.
I didn't restore their faith
in the funny books. It's my dying.
Always my dying.

Fade

Stuart talked to me in dreams so real
I believed in God for those three years.

In the first one, he knocked on the door
of my childhood home.

I came out as if I were ten again—when the world
is so fresh even the neighborhood is foreign.

We sat on the wooden porch great-grandfather
had built, our legs dangling into the front yard.

He said he was sorry for walking to California
without telling anyone. He couldn't stay

long, but wanted to say good-bye.
And everything was perfect until I glanced away.

When I looked back, his leathered face
and porcelain eyes told me

he wasn't in California.
In other dreams he confessed he killed himself

but was resurrected and fine except
for an olive-sized hole in his head,

and in others we took walks around the block,
talking about all the movies that came out after he died.

They all ended the same. Soon
I prayed for waking.

But even dead, Stuart was lonely,
so I kept him company.

In the last dream, he turned into the usual corpse
and I waited for my alarm clock.

Suddenly he became whole again,
jumped up, his brown skin renewed.

Just kidding, he said as if he were never dead.
And before I could do anything more than smile,

he waved good-bye, walked off like John Wayne
into the desert sun right before everything fades to black.

Gap

Every year, my mother reminds me
to place flowers on my sister's grave.

     On a Thursday, I buy red
     and yellow carnations
     and baby's breath. I drive alone.
     The oak that grows nearby
     has branches low enough to bear
     the graves' shadows.

     I do this
for all of us. My sister buried in Topeka.
My mother who left for Dallas. The boy
I used to be who still clings   to the years between.

I swore long ago I would never come back.
My mother does not swear,
but bears the same memories that lie beneath

Kansan green, waiting to break open
like rain on concrete. So I become
her emissary. I shoulder her burden.

I drudge down familiar streets, careful
to avoid high school crushes,
teachers, bullies, cousins who never made it out
of the state they were born in.

     By the time I've pulled onto 21st,
     the black iron gates behind,
     I think of how there is no real distance

       between anything, how Kansas
is always a breath
away. It's not the grave,
but the memory that pulls.

The Silver Age

I decide to meet the Amazing Spider-Man
at Jeremiah Bullfrogs and have a drink
for old time's sake.
He wants to know if I'll take him
back. I tell him I can't.
Not after he started courting boys
half my age. Though I knew
we never were monogamous,
I never thought he'd dump me
for a new generation of lovers.

There is always a time, dear reader,
when you're the other lover—
the new partner with young skin
and an impressionable mind.

But as years pass you find
it's only you growing
old. Your beloved hero is still
in his twenties, despite the decades
spent together. Spider-Man,
sitting in front of me, nursing a Heineken
with his mask pulled half up,
hasn't aged a day since 1977,
and here I am—
twenty-seven and already too old
to keep him company.

He brings up a young man
who lives in San Diego—

tan and thirteen and all too eager to enjoy
my old lover's stories.
He tells me I used to be that boy
and I tell him he's buying the next round.

Reading Comic Books in the Rain

The words in small white balloons
slide into each other under an ink mist

as the paper puckers. I strain my eyes
to read the slippery words aloud

to the girl who has mashed her cheek
into my wet shoulder as the world within

the cheap newsprint turns
flimsy and pulpy. Looking back, I realize

we should've stayed in that four-color world
a little longer. Escape for as long

as we could. Stave off Topeka, Kansas,
the whole goddamn world, by falling

into another one. The panels may bleed
beyond their borders, but stay contained in our hands.

The world outside bears down
like a freight train. But on that day,

a good day for reading comics,
she presses into my arm, eager to see,

and we indulge in the power
to inhabit a world a page removed from our own.

Notes

The following comics directly influenced or were directly referenced by some of the poems in this collection:

The Amazing Spider-Man #350 "Doom Service!" published in 1991, written and illustrated by David Michelinie and Erik Larsen

The Avengers #4 "Captain America Joins . . . The Avengers!" published in 1964, written and illustrated by Stan Lee and Jack Kirby

The Avengers #6 "Meet the 'Masters of Evil!'" published in 1964, written and illustrated by Stan Lee and Jack Kirby

Batman #603 "Hush, Chapter 1: The Ransom," published in 2002, written and illustrated by Jeph Loeb and Jim Lee

Batman: The Killing Joke, published in 1988, written and illustrated by Alan Moore and Brian Bolland

Marvels #4 "The Day She Died," published in 1994, written and illustrated by Kurt Busiek and Alex Ross

New X-Men (vol. 2) *#127* "Of Living and Dying," published in 2002, written and illustrated by Grant Morrison and John Paul Leon

Preacher, series published in 1995–2000, written and illustrated by Garth Ennis and Steve Dillon

Uncanny X-Men #103 "The Fall of the Tower," published in 1977, written and illustrated by Chris Claremont and Dave Cockrum

Uncanny X-Men #111 "Mindgames!" published in 1978, written and illustrated by Chris Claremont and John Byrne

Uncanny X-Men #183 "He'll Never Make Me Cry," published in 1984, written and illustrated by Chris Claremont and John Romita, Jr.

Watchmen, published in 1986–1987, written and illustrated by Alan Moore and Dave Gibbons

X-Men: God Loves, Man Kills, published in 1982, written and illustrated by Chris Claremont and Brent Anderson

Acknowledgments

Grateful acknowledgment is made to the editors of the following publications, where some of these poems originally appeared:

Magma—"Listening to Plath in Poetics"

Literary Bohemian—"Gap"

The Laurel Review—"The Secret Art of Reading a Comic"

I would also like to humbly thank the following people for their help in putting this collection together: Yusef Komunyakaa, Alison Meyers, and everyone at Cave Canem for reading my work and giving me a chance. Jeff Shotts, Katie Dublinski, and the Graywolf Press crew for giving it life. And many thanks to the following people for their guidance and support: Kyle Churney, Amy Fleury, Lisa Gill, Joy Harjo, Mary Power, Christina Yovovich, and a special thanks to Lisa D. Chavez who worked tirelessly with me on this collection in its early stages.

Finally, I'd like to thank Lisa Hase, who always knew the right things to say, the right things to cut and to keep, and her unending support all these years.

Gary Jackson is the winner of the 2009 Cave Canem Poetry Prize for his first book, *Missing You, Metropolis*. He was born and raised in Topeka, Kansas, and received his Master of Fine Arts degree in poetry from the University of New Mexico in 2008. His poems have appeared in *inscape, Literary Bohemian, Magma,* and small chapbooks. He has been a fierce lover of comics for nearly twenty years.

Book design by Rachel Holscher.
Composition by BookMobile Design and Publishing Services, Minneapolis, Minnesota.
Manufactured by BookMobile on acid-free 30 percent postconsumer wastepaper.